the
letters
I **will**
never
send.

the letters I will never send.

isabella dorta

Andrews McMeel
PUBLISHING®

Andrews McMeel Publishing
a division of Andrews McMeel Universal
1130 Walnut Street, Kansas City, Missouri 64106

www.andrewsmcmeel.com

23 24 25 26 27 VEP 10 9 8 7 6 5 4 3 2 1

ISBN: 978-1-5248-8882-4

Library of Congress Control Number: 2023938031

Editor: Patty Rice
Art Director/Designer: Brittany Lee
Production Editor: Jennifer Straub
Production Manager: Shona Burns

ATTENTION: SCHOOLS AND BUSINESSES

Andrews McMeel books are available at quantity discounts with bulk purchase for educational, business, or sales promotional use. For information, please e-mail the Andrews McMeel Publishing Special Sales Department: sales@amuniversal.com.

to myself.

to the old me,
the broken girl with a shaken heart
and bruised fingertips.

to the girl who wrote these letters.

a
note
from
the
author

hello again, you.

please excuse me, but before you rush into reading, i have a few things i must explain.

now, this *book* is not the sort of thing you just read once and put down. truthfully i am not sure if this collection of writings even deserves the loose title of *book;* it is remarkably different to anything i have written before. this *book* is a collection of letters.

i want you to do what i could not, what i wish i was brave enough to commit to. these letters thus far have remained unsent. i want you to change that for me.

the purpose of the publication of this *book* is for you to send these letters to whoever you think deserves them; post them anonymously through letterboxes, scatter them from rooftops, send them with your name attached, create art from them, burn them, stick them to your walls, rip out each page that your heart calls for. they are yours to use, yours to decide their purpose, yours to destroy. do what i did not and make sure they are read by whoever they are intended for.

just like last time, there will be no capital letters. remember that no letter should hold more weight than the next. in each letter, there is power.

there are mentions of ugly things and traumatic life experiences. please guard your heart, do look after yourself, and if suicide, sexual assault, eating disorders, or childhood abuse are things that may trigger you, read with caution. skip some pages if they may do more harm than good. for chapters addressed directly to your traumas, remember that there comes a time when these letters should be sent. use these letters as a means of reaching out for help. send them to family members, friends, therapists, or loved ones you trust and let these letters say everything you may be too afraid to. these letters are written in first person, so read them and send them as if you had written them. at the back of this *book* you will find a section called "your letters" and i have left it blank for you to fill. use them to write your own letters and send them out into the world in just the same way.

make sure these pages are loved and cared for, but most of all, make sure they are read.

as always, my darling,

thank you,

and enjoy.

to
the
universe

to the universe

although i don't believe in god,
i like to think there is someone watching over me.

i'd take an eight-year-old at a science fair
holding my existence
in their sticky hands.
a fluke experiment
and an accidental existence.

but i'd so prefer some sort of *being*,
one who is undoubtedly proud
of what i have achieved with their help.

i like to imagine they giggle fondly at me
whenever i ask for something
they know would be bad for me,
like a dog who begs for chocolate.

"oh.
silly girl," they smile,
"you really have no idea that
this could kill you,
do you?"

to the universe

does someone love me
yet?

i hope so.

i hope their warmth
has woven its way
into the cracks of my heart
and glued me back together.

do they treat me well?

do they want to marry me?

do they stroke my head to sleep at night?

does someone love me,
universe?

am i loved
yet?

to the universe

i think the most beauty is held in things that cause
    pain.
it's the way we beg our bodies to climb mountains
just for the view,
or swim in deep waters for the thrill of it.
we jump out of planes
and love bad people
and bask in the sun
and stare at stars.
we like things that could kill us
and yet
i don't think i would have it any other way.
there is a certain comfort in danger,
in unhappiness
and loneliness.
there is undoubtedly
the most beauty in the things we don't quite
    understand
but marvel anyway.
and i love that.

to the universe

i can't keep begging you, universe.
please,
let me see him again,
even if it is only in my dreams
(and for a split second at that)
please let him return to me.
i know he isn't good for me
but
neither is living like this.
i can't remain on my knees in front of you forever.
just grant me
this.
let me see
for myself

one
last
time

how terrible he is to me.
let me learn
from my own mistakes
again
and again
and again
and again
and—
please, universe . . .

please.

to the universe

i hope the moon finds as much comfort in me
as i do in her.
i hope she spends the daytime thinking of me,
waiting for me to emerge into her darkness
and bask in the little light she sheds.
i wonder if she even knows
what she means to me.
if she knows i have worn her image around my neck
for the last five years
and how i refuse to tell anyone why.
it is our secret.
my ode to her,
and how she is the
often overlooked,
often overcast.
i hope she looks down at me
as i look up at her
and knows i would pick her over the sun
every
single
day.

to the universe

i like the rain.

i like the wind at night.

i like what i imagine dusk tastes of
(honeysuckle and sweetness).

i like mundanity and how unusually pretty it is.

i like star signs and astrology and plants and
all the hippy dippy shit
my exes used to hate.

i like tea light lanterns
and freckles that have been sun-kissed.

i like rushed ballpoint drawings on the backs
of coffee shop napkins.

i like kisses that taste of my favorite cigarettes.

i like living.

i like happiness.

i like feeling
completely
and
utterly
in bliss.

i like what the universe has blessed me with.

to the universe

i think i am afraid of never being loved again.

and i am <u>so damn scared</u> of saying that out loud,
in case the universe latches onto it
and makes it true.

i think i am more afraid that the
half-assed, "i-can't-be-bothered" love you gave me
is all i will ever get.

maybe—
maybe i should've said "thank you"
for the half of your heart i was given.
i should be grateful the universe granted me that.

i suppose being half-loved is better than nothing,
because now that i do not even have that,
i feel more alone than i ever have before

and i find myself talking to the universe,
pleading,
not to be loved fully,
nor even for half of a lover.

i ask the universe if she will grant me a quarter perhaps.

to the universe

i know it is for the best, universe,
that you have not returned him to me.
but,
you should know,
the day that i am given the opportunity,
i will clasp onto him tightly with two hands
and i cannot promise that i will let go.
and i know that is why you keep him out of my reach.
unfortunately though,
you do not stop me from thinking of him.
and so he is *just grazed* by the tips of my fingers,
he is close enough to smell
and far enough away to spare myself the heartache.
you dangle him in front of me
in memories and pictures
like a carrot and a stupid donkey, universe.
is that all i am to you?
i guess it is true that i am driven pathetically by love.
so much so,
that i often think
if i can just stretch out far enough,
graze him for long enough,
i might be able to reach for him.
but like i said,
i cannot promise i would let go,
so it is probably for the best
that you keep him out of reach,
right, universe?

to the universe

on nights like this,
where i cannot bear to hold myself any longer
and my arms have grown weary from trying,
i step outside.
i think it is the peacefulness i enjoy most,
how empty the world feels and how full i feel
to have a friend in the night sky.
someone who never leaves
and seems to always look down on me fondly.
i adore her
and the way she shivers in silver.
she lets me bathe
in her glow.
iridescently.
happily.
effortlessly.

to the universe

please tell me i can be happy.
to be truthful
it is all i can dream of
and i'm not sure if
i can keep existing like this.

my heart is not even on my sleeve,
it is worn like a collector's item by the boys who
mistreated me.
will i be whole again?
please tell me i can be.
i *must* be.
please.

to the universe

my cup is half filled,
half empty,
half missing something,
and i don't quite know what it is,
but i know i am yearning for it.

i want to feel full
and warm
and happy
and like i belong.
i want to fit into this world
and i want the world to fit me, too.

i am desperate to live life properly
without caution or regret
and i don't know how yet
but i am trying to teach myself.

i am a toddler removing my own training wheels.
i have fallen
and fallen
and fallen,
but i am getting back up

and i am trying.

to
my
family

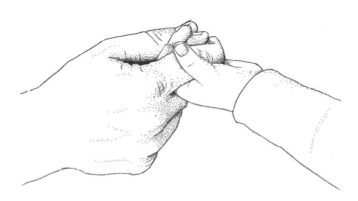

to my family

you taught me to be me.
every time my heart was shattered,
yours did too,

but that never stopped you
from picking up each of my shards,
bloodying your own hands

and piecing me back together.
if eve was designed from adam's rib,
a daughter must be designed from a mother's soul

and you have done everything
in your power
to protect mine.

selflessly kind,
selfishly protective.
i am indebted to you for your guidance.

thank you. truly, endlessly,
thank you
for teaching me how to be me.

to my family

the day you died physically,
i died figuratively.
i felt coldness creep into my bones
and a softness leave my heart.
i felt myself harden
with sadness and sorrow and a disgust for living.
i didn't know how to exist without you,
without someone to tell my secrets to
or complain about my bad days to.

and it is so fucking unfair.
i hate myself
for hating mourning
but i do not know what else to feel.
it is devastating
and heartbreaking
and i am so sorry to make this about me,
to turn your passing into my pity,
but without you here to comfort me,
i cannot exist as anything but broken.
i miss you more and more every day.
i expect it will be like this until i see you again,
in another lifetime,
in another world,
in another life.

to my family

i don't think you realize quite
how brilliant you are.
you hold more compassion than most and
trust me
when i tell you,
i know this is nothing short of truthful.
you are rare
in your unwavering compassion.
and that is commendable.

to my family

when you held me for the first time,
when i looked up at you
like you were my whole world
and you looked down at me
like i had just been born into yours,
i wonder if you felt your heart explode.

there's something so ethereal about a mother's love,
how pure and unconditional it is.
you learned to love me
for nine months
before we ever even met
and
i have spent eighteen years
perfecting how to return the favor.

i bet you spent hours
imagining me vividly.
did i turn out like you expected?
are my eyes as blue as you pictured?
my heart as kind as you hoped for?

i hope i have made you proud
and i hope to only make you prouder
as our lives go on.

to my family

there is comfort
in having someone listen.
trust me,
i have spent years searching for exactly that,
a person with open years and an open heart
but my trauma has fallen on deaf ears
and
cold stares
and
"have you tried telling them how you feel?"
"maybe you should just chill out a bit."
i thought i would never find someone who cared
enough to listen, and to help

until i reached out to you.
and i get that you've been here the entire time,
silently waiting until i was ready to confide in you,
but god,
you make me feel so much less alone
and so much more normal.
so
thank you
for listening to me.

to my family

the woman who raised me,
who singlehandedly watered me,
placed me in sunlight,
and allowed me to flourish
is the woman that i owe everything to.
thank you,
mum.
thank you.

to

my

best

friend

to my best friend

i think there is a difference
between friendship
and what we have.

you are the type of person
i have always wanted in my life.
i have searched
for a person like you
for a very long time.

and i know that now i have finally found you,
i will never let you go.

to my best friend

you are the type of person
who will only ever show me
that you love me
in the strangest of ways.
not in gifts, in actions, or in smiles.
no words are ever said.
you do not need them.
you just seem to know
exactly how to silently say
that it is us against the world.

and you are the type of person who,
frustratingly,
does not know how to accept my love.
you brush it off but
the strings of my heart so adore you.
they are tied so tightly with yours
entwined with trust and laughter
and the memories of a million moments
that i know i will never forget.

you are the type of person who,
without even trying,
can brighten my whole mood.
you are brilliant
and weird
and difficult
and frustrating
and i would not change you for the world.

to my best friend

my best friend
does not see her own beauty,

but she is the prettiest thing
in my world

and i am so saddened
that she does not realize this.

the day that she does
will be the day

that i hug her
the tightest i ever have.

she is so much more
than what strangers can see,

and a mirror will never do her justice,
because it does not show her

the true beauty
that her heart holds.

to my best friend

i wish you could see yourself
in the same light i see you in.
this warm yellow glow that matches the fire
in your eyes *so well.*
and trust me
when i say
that i am yet to meet anyone else
with eyes that can both
heal and burn so badly.

you are the embodiment of power.

you are the light that bleeds through morning curtains,
coaxing from beds,
and basking those who need it in your glow.
a touch midas would be envious of,
you are the epitome of beauty.

you are compassion unmatched,
with your fleeting moments
where you disappear from my night
to bring someone else morning.
i know it pains you to leave me
in darkness
but if you had ever turned around to look,
you would witness my
contented goodbye.
it is in your absence that i realize
beauty means nothing if it is not seen.

you are the sole child of strength and resilience
and i know you have your muted days,
where your furious burn becomes a cautious caress,
dulled and hidden behind your darkening clouds,
but this softness is what made me fall in love with you.
it is human
and it is pure
and it is *you.*

to my best friend

i relish in the prospect that one day
you will understand how people stare at you,
with a gaze half filled of awe
and half filled of gentle jealousy.

please,
do not dull yourself for fear of blinding others.
my darling,
that is what sunglasses are for;
to protect eyes from girls
who unapologetically beam.

and my god,
you beam.

to my best friend

i longed for you.
most days,
i spent my free time looking for you
just hoping i would stumble across you so that
i didn't need to be
alone
anymore.

i envisioned us completing one another,
offering unwavering support
and a friendship that you see
only in films.
i hoped to meet you soon
pleaded for us to become unrelated family.
it is embarrassing to admit
but i planned out how i'd first say hello
how i'd hold you when your heart was broken,
how you'd smile at me as we completed life together.

although,
i have to admit,
i never quite believed i would find you,
and so you can imagine my surprise
when i did,
or,
rather,
when you found me.

i like to think you dreamt of a friend like me
in the way i did of you.
i hope i am everything you imagined.

you most certainly are to me.

to my best friend

unapologetic
and unashamed.
that is how we love.

i must tell you, child,
there was a time i was embarrassed of my intensity,
perturbed in the way
i held undeserving men emotionally.
now,
i am unequivocally undoubting.

my darling,
these men have never deserved us
in all of our
zealousness.
they cannot hold us still,
let alone under their thumbs
for long enough to control us.

girls like us do not sit pretty,
uneventfully loving,
gingerly,
from a distance.

we do not recoil at raised voices,
or give way to a man's love.

we do not collapse.

not easily,
anyway.

it must be frightening for them,
i suppose,
for us to embrace every part of them,
the bits they do not like,
the bits no one has acknowledged before,
the bits of their hearts no one has touched before.

but,
let me comfort you with this,
expect to be forever coated in his mind,
present, even when we are not

because we—
we are <u>not</u> the sort of girls
they can
easily
forget.

to
my
crush

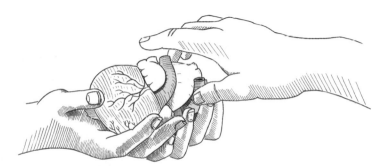

to my crush

oh. my love.

you do know
you are a force to be reckoned with,
don't you?

and you do know
i've always fancied my chances
with men who are
more storm and
less drizzle.

and if you don't already,
i think you *should know*
that i would quite happily
let you consume me in your downpour,
as long as i am allowed to hold your hand

while you ruin me
with the dangerous love
i know we both
crave.

oh, my love.

to my crush

i think i knew as soon as i met you, when i saw how
your eyes lit up as they caught mine and the way that
smile crept onto your face before you could nervously
suppress it. i think i knew i would love you one day.
(and i was right.)

i fell in love with you quickly, the way you don't realize
the tide has come in until your feet are wet and you're
belly laughing with friends; the way you get caught in a
storm without an umbrella during the middle of july;
the way you wake early in a bid to watch the sunrise,
but before you know it, you are bathed in light and
have begun to appreciate the beauty of the world
through sleep-filled eyes.

i loved you quickly and uncomfortably and
unapologetically and i always will. i know you will, too;
i saw it the day that i met you. i saw it in your eyes as
you caught mine and i unintentionally smiled right back
at you, just before i gathered the courage to say hello.

to my crush

i see myself marrying you, you silly boy,
and you don't even know it.

but not yet.

we have to wait a little bit
until i am sure it'll work,
because if it doesn't,
oh.
god, it'll break us both.
you silly boy.

to my crush

i said i would wait for you and i meant it,
i will.

but waiting implies there is an end.
and i am not so sure that there ever will be with you.

i think i may have become your fall-back plan
a "just-in-case-everything-else-doesn't-work-out" plan

and it really fucking sucks
but i promised i would wait

and so i will
patiently.

to my crush

if i choose to love you now
i will have to choose to un-love you later.
i have to do it first,
before you stop loving me because,
if i don't,
if you stop loving me first,
i know i will not be able to cope.
i am petrified of heartbreak
and of losing the one thing i was so scared to accept in
the first place.
i guard my heart,
because if i don't,
i am scared i will lose it again.

and i'm not so sure i will be able to find it this time.

to my crush

she waltzed in,
later than usual for her,
and slumped into the corner of the room next to me.

she smelled of cigarettes and fruit,
like this juxtaposition of sourness and sweetness
that seemed to match her just right.
she was a walking contradiction.

this girl was infuriating,
i mean, *really infuriating.*

she flicked a stray curl of red
over her shoulder toward me
and stared at me.
a bored expression on her face at whatever nonsense
the teacher was spouting.

neither of us paid any attention.
i just stared back at her.

fucking.
infuriating.

i couldn't take my eyes off of her.

to my crush

for you,
i would be a fool ten times over,

if you'd let me.

(and probably if you didn't anyway.)

to my crush

when you tell me you love me for the first time,

promise me you will not say it
during sex,
i do not want our lips to part for a single second.

promise me you will not say it
when we are drunk on tequila and lime,
when the salt has coated our mouths
and i can taste it with every kiss we share.

promise me you will not say it
when we are out for dinner,
spending money we do not have,
eating food too expensive for its own good.

promise me you will not say it
when I am sleeping next to you,
unable to memorize the curls of your lips
as you
whisper it,
too dark to see the tears on our faces.

promise me you will not say it
on valentine's day,
or birthdays,
or easter,
or christmas.

please
do not ruin these things for me.

when you tell me you love me,
make it mundane,
make it uneventful,
make it like we've been saying it for a thousand years.

because
when you stop saying it,
i do not want to be reminded of it every time
i kiss someone new,
or i smell citrus, or i eat out, or i fall asleep, or on any
holidays at all.
please.

do not taint my life with your love
and then your absence of it.

to my crush

i really do miss being held
and i'd quite like to be loved again.
loved loudly.
i would like to taste your happiness every time we kiss.
&
i would love you just the same.
perhaps louder even.

if that's okay with you.

to my crush

i am unexplainably difficult.
i am easy enough to fall in love with
but god,
once i have you,
i promise you
you will regret giving me your heart.

i will not ever think i am deserving of your love
so i will discard it
even though i begged for it.

i'm so sorry.
i just can't help myself.

to my crush

i tell you i'm a poet
and you ask
"well what would you write about me?"

you see,
nobody has ever asked me that before
and so i find my brain flicking through pages of my
notebooks.
the coffee-stained napkins
and hasty scribbles.
i search every corner of my brain
for an effortless line to show you how serious i am.

until i realize,
i have never written a poem about anyone the way i
would about you.
i have described eyes
and sloping noses
and careful fingers on collarbones,

but i am yet to write about the person whose soul
reminds me of clouds
with linings so lucid
they catch the light in the way i imagine your hands
would catch my heart.

i am missing lines that describe my fingers tracing the
braille of your skin,
how i will read your past and our future through touch,
blind to anything but our love.

i never realized my poetry was unfinished
until i met you,
now i look at every piece as incomplete
and with gaps that before i had not seen as empty.

i wonder if that is because our love is infinite
or if i will be forever placing ink onto paper

writing endlessly to preserve what we have
and trying to find you again and again
between my god-awful handwriting.

so if our initial introduction to each other's love
happens across metaphors
and hyperboles,
if it means i do not have to take
a single breath without you,
my darling,
my hands will never not be covered in ink stains and
your fingerprints.

i never told you this,
but it took me three days
to uncover the courage to talk to you,
even longer to craft the script
i was so determined to use.

it was something like:

"hi. i know this sounds ridiculous but i think i'm going to love you someday and i think you are going to love me too."

how incredibly cliche and romantically charged of me.

i'm glad your eyes seemed scarier up close
because when i stuttered through the "hi,"
too starstruck to carry on,
you found it endearing
and i completely forgot
whatever poetic love declaration i had written
in my back pocket anyway.

although,
i do like to think you're not the sort
to be scared off

by a stranger's love.
i don't see you as someone skittish of how loud my
vulnerable love can be.
i know i will love you unapologetically,
with teardrops for jewelry
and you as my necklace
so that i will never have to feel
my heart beat alone against just my chest again.

i know i will write feverishly to preserve what we have.

"i don't know yet," i say,
"but i know it will be the best poem
that i could ever hope to write."

to my crush

i kind of love that i noticed you first
that i had the privilege of letting my eyes roam your
face
before you even knew mine existed.

you see i always knew you were out there
somewhere
i just had to find you to love you
i never stopped searching.

to my crush

i don't kiss and tell,
but if you were to lay your lips on mine,

my heart would never stop shouting about it.

to
my
lover

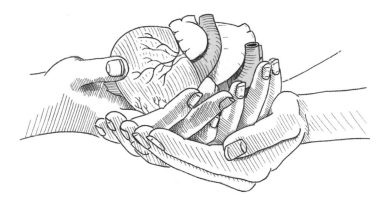

to my lover

there was just something about him.
i could never quite put my finger on what it was
exactly,
but i knew there was something.
it drew me into him,

he dizzied me with his scent,
softened me in his arms,
quietened my heart.

don't get me wrong,
it raced when i was near him,
but quietly
as if it was afraid of scaring him away,
afraid of startling a boy who was skittish around girls
whose hearts spoke louder than themselves.

i am not timid,
but for him i felt my insides shy
and my stomach hide up into my mouth.
i was desperate for his approval,
his affection.
it was an unrequited desire to be wanted.
or so i thought.

one day,
as he fell asleep on the phone to me,
he asked me to describe

why i was falling in love with him,
i heard his heart beat just as quickly as mine,
but quieten in the same way,
as he lay the phone on his chest.

and so i told him.
i strung together sentences of admiration and want.
he listened.
chuckled.
asked for more.

i said:
"there's just something about you."
he asked what.
i said:
"i do not know yet."

between you and me,
that wasn't quite the truth.
the "something" was my reflection in his eyes,
the way we mirrored our insecurities
from previous lovers
and the way we both silently agreed to heal together.

an unspoken bond of past trauma
and the hope of a healed future.

i will dry his tears.
he will dry mine.

to my lover

it was a summer of red wine,
high pollen counts,
exposed thighs,
and vanilla lip balm.

i always liked how you tasted of baked goods
and spoke with a voice far sweeter than frosting,
ever so slightly raspy from our shared marlboros.

sometimes you wore tank tops so i could think about
how soft your skin was.
there was a freckle i liked to trace, on your left
shoulder.

i don't think you ever realized quite what i was doing.
i was letting my fingers memorize you,
let the imprint of yourself be buried
between my fingerprints.
unique and beautiful and combined.

between kisses
you told me your dna will live inside my mouth
for the next six months,
to remember this when i miss you,
when i have nothing else of you left.
i said,
"not if you kiss me again."

come december you were gone,
but my fingertips still remember you.

sometimes,
i trace my own left shoulder
and that makes me feel *a little bit less crazy.*

to my lover

i fell in love with you for the first time
when you held my hand in that park

when i watched the sun set in between watching you
and i saw how beautiful your eyes looked
illuminated by purples and yellows.

i fell in love with you for the second time
when you brought me up from one knee,
kissed me hard,
and told me you wanted to marry me, too.

when i saw how unfalteringly happy you looked to
spend the rest of your life with me.

the third time was at the end of the aisle
as you leaned in for our first official kiss and i saw how
beautiful you looked in white

when you held our baby for the first time.

when you held our second.

when you held our third.

i fall in love with you over and over
at every chance i get,
at every life milestone we complete together
and every new moment becomes my favorite.
(until the next, that is.)
for as long as i am with you
i know i will forever find a new reason
to become besotted.
i love you endlessly and purely and
as beautifully as you are.
always,
my love.
always.

to my lover

come and kiss me.
hard.
then softly.
then tell me how much you love the freckles
under my left eye.
trace them.
kiss me again.
lay with me.
let us be pure and captivating
and let us be each other's.

to my lover

i placed my head between her shoulder and her neck and inhaled. *oh.* she smelled like warm rain and thunder, the sort you wouldn't be angry to be drenched in.

i think she eventually consumed me in the same way i used to get caught in the rain, pitifully quickly and day-dreaming of sunshine. although, on occasion, i have been known to enjoy storms and their blindsiding brazenness.

i like the way they are not embarrassed or bashful. i like how they are unapologetic in the symphony they create, with every raindrop playing the violin strings of spiders' homes or drumming on rooftops like we deserve to hear nothing less.

i like the way it is unpredictably eventful, how it graces summers with its presence and ruins autumns with its absence. that bit is especially like her.

eventually, i learned to rush outside whenever it was forecast to rain, desperate to experience something that would remind me of her. that sort of rain always seems to taste of her lips. and cherries, but maybe that's just my imagination.

i still love the smell though. warm rain and thunder.
electric and heavy air, the sort that weighs down on you
until you realize there is nowhere else you would
rather be anyway.

i guess the smell of overpowering-ness has always
made my knees weak.

and she smelled beautifully of it.

to my lover

kiss me
like you used to,
if you remember how it felt
when we were young,
stupid kids,
how it felt to have our lips belong to each other.
i miss the cluelessness and the clunkiness.
kiss me
like you are trying to relive us.

to my lover

mint and cigarettes.

that's what he told me i tasted like.

this mixture of early mornings and danger.
peppermint
and
smoke.
i couldn't help but wonder what she tasted like,
what he had assigned as her flavor
and i wondered what his tastebuds preferred.

i think i always knew deep down
that the taste of his first love would
never quite leave his lips,
trust me,
i have tasted its overpowering-ness myself.
but i have always wondered if i am able to replace it
with something sweeter,
something
smokier,

something mintier.

he hates smoking,
but he has told me how he always likes the taste of it
on my lips.
he never stops trying to savor me.

i'm still trying to work out what he tastes of.
i don't know quite what it is yet
but my tastebuds
already long for it.

to my lover

i think loving you was both the kindest
and most self-destructive thing i have ever done.

in the same breath,
we built new bridges and burned old ones.

you were a person i found and misplaced simultaneously,
and i wonder whether that means i have won or lost.

i guess this is something i will not know
until our time has run out.

until i have either grown old with you or lost you.
(i hope it is the former and not the latter.)

loving you was the best thing i think that has ever
happened to me.

and also sort of the worst.
but if you have taught me anything,

it is that i should take the good with the bad,
and so i will love you,

unafraid of losing you
until either i cannot love you anymore,

or you will not let me.
whichever comes first.

to my lover

i did warn you,
on our third date,
as we lay together
tangled in each other's skin and creased linen,
i warned you i would be difficult to love.

and you laughed
and told me
boys like you
were born with a free-roaming heart
for girls like me
with caged ones.

you told me you would chip away at my stone
and you would help me heal.

i smiled.
it was the perfect response.
you knew that it was.
i had hoped that it was nothing but truthful
but like most things,
only time will tell.

to my lover

i hope you still think i am pretty
when you see me collapse for the first time.
when you watch me crumble
and disappear
and disappoint you.

i hope you like to kiss my cheeks
when they are wet and
when i stop pretending i am okay.

i hope you stroke my hair
when i try to melt into your body heat
because being by myself
is a bit too cold sometimes.

i hope you—
i hope—
i—
i just hope you—

(please don't leave me.)

to my lover

i begged for someone to find me,
to be the person someone loved entirely
and purely.
there was a time that i thought it was hopeless.
unachievable.
until you stumbled into my life.
and after being hurt so many times,
i relished in the idea *you might not.*
you might be different.

sometimes, though,
when i cannot will myself to think of happy things,
my brain tells me stories of you leaving me.
on mornings where i wake up alone,
shaking and scared of my accidental manifestations,
i think *if i leave now,*
before you have the chance to break me,
i may spare myself this healing.
i may find myself in fewer pieces than if i stay.

i hope i am wrong.
i hope this will not end in another hurt—
you have assured me
it won't.
but then again,
so did all of the others.

to my lover

i knew as soon as i met you
that we were cut from the same cloth
reversed designs but we still seemed to match in an
uncomfortable way.
our love was filled with fire
and unruly determination
and quietness
and unspeakable noise
and opposites that attract.
we really were the biggest cliché, weren't we?
even so—
even through the conflict
i'd still choose you any day of the week,
even if i know it isn't good for either of us.
with a love like ours,
perhaps we were meant to grow separately first
and meet later.
but we didn't.
and so now we're stuck in this limbo.
caught between wanting to be together but not being
healed enough to do so.
ah.
what a beautiful, romantic mess.

to my lover

i finally had that feeling again.
it only lasted for a few seconds
and as soon as i looked away from his eyes
i felt my cheeks flush with embarrassment,

but it felt beautifully raw
to feel my heart leap into my head
as they agreed
to never make me choose between them again.

i didn't think i would ever feel this way after
that last love.

maybe this time the feeling will learn to stay.
maybe it won't be so fleeting.
maybe,
when i'm with him,
i'll learn to love it again.

to
my
ex

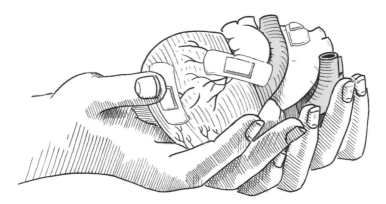

to my ex

you'll come back to me one day,
and it probably won't work again,
the way a broken clock is coincidentally right
twice a day.
maybe our second go at it
will be just that.
an accidental afternoon
where the right time is displayed once again.
i'll probably embrace it,
try to stretch out that minute
for as long as possible.
i'll know it's fated not to last.

to my ex

you were never my right person
at the wrong time.
no, if you were my right person
you would have told me that
time was a social construct
and a bullshit excuse anyway.
you would have loved me in spite of time.

to my ex

from
friends
to
lovers
to
strangers (*who can't look at each other for too long
without feeling our hearts burst and our heads fill with
memories of stupid romantic bullshit that really was
never how we imagined it anyway because the idea of
each other was so much better than the reality we
lived*)
to
nothing.

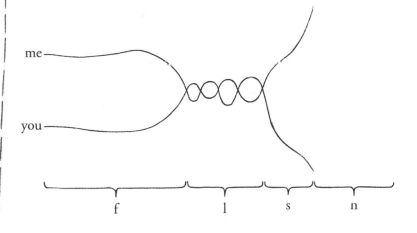

to my ex

and i am just so angry still.

i'm so angry
at the fact that you just manage to move on
so easily.

you swept me up.
every memory,

every moment spent together,
every piece of me you had,
and you pushed it into a corner.

you told me it was almost like you put me into a box,
closed the lid, and just forgot about me.

after everything,
everything we did together,
all our plans for our future,
you somehow managed to walk away
without having to feel
a thing.

and it makes me so angry.
it makes me so angry
because i could never do the same to you.

my mind is littered with you,
you touched every part of my heart,
you rooted yourself deep in every aspect of my life;

i see you everywhere.

and i have never felt a rage like this.

to my ex

i guess distance does not make the heart grow fonder,
right?

or rather,

i guess distance does not make *your* heart grow fonder,

only mine.

to my ex

so another man broke my heart. i'm assuming this
means another six sessions with a therapist, once i decide
i'm deserving of healing, that is. the only silver lining
is that this boy didn't cloud my love nearly as much as
the last, or the one before him. they all treat me the
same way though—badly, and with no regard for my
heart. they stamp on it, as if just walking away from me
wasn't enough, they like to make sure i feel their feet as
they leave. and i am so fucked. i have footprints on my
heart and their only purpose is identifiability for the
next man, to show him i am easily hurt. i must stink of
attachment issues and naive trust. my eyes show
nothing but stupidity and i think that must be why men
love it when i stare up at them. they have broken me,
one by one. i asked to be ruined and they obliged—
grinning and smiling with excitement. regardless of all
this shit, the really bad bit of this all, the bit i can only
admit in writing, is that when these men break me, i
mourn you again. i think of you and how i never loved
them in the same way. i think of how if it were you,
instead of them, i wouldn't even bat an eyelid. i would
let you treat me however you'd like as long as it meant
you wouldn't leave again. because if i knew which
butterfly flapping its wings caused you to leave and
caused the permanent mass extinction of its ancestors
in my stomach, i would spend years inventing time
travel just to go back and pull each fucking wing off in
the hopes it may mean you stay with me. i am in as
many pieces right now as that monarch would be, i can

assure you. and all that i want—all that i need—
is *a hug*.
preferably *from you*.

my therapist says this is all so silly.
maybe it is,
but god i won't stop thinking of it.

to my ex

i could write you thousands of letters.

but you know that,

don't you?

you know you're my favorite muse.

to my ex

i don't know if i'll ever truly get away from you,
because the second i think i'm free
and moving on,
i'll smell your aftershave
lingering in my room,
or hear our song on the radio,
or remember how you used to hold me
when someone else tries to.

i really hate that i can't stop thinking about you,
or writing about you.
how sad it all is,
that all you are now
is a distant memory
i use as a writing prompt
instead of the person
who i was
so deeply in love with.

to my ex

and in our parting moments,
in those last few words exchanged,
you told me to never change myself for anyone else.

i don't think you ever quite realized
the irony in that sentence.
maybe you just didn't see how much
i had changed myself for you
or maybe you thought that
that version of me was better,
that the "me" you met
didn't deserve to return.

and now i am beginning to wonder
just who you meant by "anyone else,"
because i know sure as shit
i will never love anyone again
and i am sure as shit
you must know that, too.
you must see how i can never repair my heart.
so who did you mean?
did you mean me? did you mean:
"don't change yourself for you"?
is it that i am not worthy of healing the broken me?

i think you liked me most when i was a shell of myself,
a casualty from our war.
maybe it makes you feel powerful to know you can ruin
the girl who was so besotted by you.
ruin her
so badly,
she cannot leave her house without vomiting
or without clutching at her own palms.

so okay,
i'll try not to change. maybe you'll like me again if i
just do as you say.
one. last. time.

to my ex

i think even if you came back,
if you ever decided
that you wanted to,
i think i'd still be disappointed.

i'd probably try to kiss your lips
as if nothing has happened,
hold the back of your neck
or your face.

i bet you'd taste different.
maybe you'd kiss me differently,
not with the overwhelming hunger you used to
but this new softness.

i don't know if i like softness.

to my ex

you had an insatiable appetite

and i just never seemed to fill you up.

to my ex

we were never meant to last.
we were killing time, the way young kids often do,
trying to find any weak reason to wake up the next
morning.
trying to discover the sun
and face it on bad days where we cannot exist
without at least a little bit of light.

and i know how cliché that must've sounded
to everyone else
i know it's stupid and nonsensical
but it made perfect sense to us.
and a lot of our relationship was like that,
no one else got it but us.
we existed together
in the collision
of the confusion
of everyone around us.

sort of like,

you know how when you catch a glimpse of a
car crash about to happen
and you can't help but stare as you drive past
with bated breath and half a heart
or

when you watch a child fall in slow motion, about to
scrape their knees so badly, so painfully,
and you wait to see how violently
their cries will ring in your ears
or

when you accidentally stumble across
an overly, unnecessarily graphic scene in a movie
that most definitely will be enough to trigger you but
technically
they haven't quite shown anything too explicit yet

and you want to look away
but your body won't let you.

because your eyes are drawn to the danger of what
almost wasn't?

that was us.

except with us, i guess,
there was no almost
and no one looked away.
they just watched us destroy each other.
implode in our young naive puppy love.

it ended sadly, horribly.
it was the sort of tragedy i never wanted to write about
but here i am.

once again,
i cannot help but vomit our story onto pages of
weak scribbles and tear-drop stains.
i am regurgitating our truth so pitifully
it is embarrassing.

neither of us actually died,
not technically.
we are still breathing through
damaged lungs and broken rib cages.
our love existed in shared cigarettes and hearts
that were so full our bodies could no longer close.

we are bandaged with trauma
and stained gauze
and each other.
and we always will be.

six days out of the week
i only woke up because of him.
six days out of the week

he only woke up because of me.
those seventh days,
those were always the hardest.
they were the days we could not exist for each other
anymore.

those were the days of danger that were *almost*
not "almost"s.

to my ex

and if you ever find yourself wanting to talk to me again,
thumbs poised over my name
a message half-typed out,
don't hesitate.
do not wait another month, another minute.
if you ever find yourself wanting to come back to me,
know that i have been waiting for you to since the day
you left.

i will always be waiting for you.

to my ex

i remember being so excited to love you.
i remember the first time you said it to me,

how you looked at me,
how i was so impatient to hear it,

how i forced the moment to come early
but somehow—

somehow
it was still so perfect for us.

i wonder if you ever meant it,
or if you just said it out of ease.

i meant it,
always.

and i wish i didn't,
because it would've been so much easier.

and you never told me when exactly
you stopped loving me,

but i just sort of knew.
you stopped saying it with that look in your eyes,

or with that smile.
it became rushed,

it became "goodbye" instead of "hello,"
you mumbled it,

you looked away,

you
just
stopped
saying
it.

i'd give anything to hear you say it again.

to my ex

and once again,
i am just too much
and someone else is just too little.
another disappointment, another expectation not lived
up to,
another promise broken.
and so many empty words.
god,
you made me think you were falling in love with me.
what bullshit.
this isn't the first time this has happened,
and it probably won't be the last.
you won't be the last man to tell me
i am just *too good* for you.

to my ex

hazel eyes
then gray
then blue.
maybe i'm collecting them,
the glossy shards of eyes from the boys that have
broken me.
i'll create a mosaic out of you all,
a pretty stained-glass window.
i'll cut myself in the process
jagged and
bloody and
stuck together with poor excuses.
a jigsaw of brokenness and trauma.
i just need a green and a brown
to complete my little project
of heartache and abuse.

to my ex

i wanted us to work so badly.
oh, god, i would have laid my life on the line.
a sacrificial ritual of adoration,
i would have done anything for you.
anything to make you stay with me.

oh, baby,
you knew this.

to my ex

you told me you loved me for the first time between
kisses.
between the words
"you're so beautiful" and
"i mean it."
i almost crashed my car on the way home.
you told me it a second time
a month later
between white sheets and pale, freckled skin
all breath and sweetness
carefully unplanned.

we broke up in the same place we met,
the same place we first kissed,
the same place you told me you loved me.
how like me that is,
to latch onto a place and dress its mundanity in
romance.
i've always loved bittersweet endings
and soured goodbyes.
and "i love you"s,
in between kisses.

to my ex

i prayed to god that you'd return to me
and you did,
but i don't think he was the one who sent you.
there's a reason they tell you to not pray out loud
but my love,
i would let you drag me straight to hell
if i got to hold your hand all the way down.

and i will forever reach for you
the way the ocean constantly kisses the shore
regardless of the sand's indifference.
desperate for acknowledgment
and appreciation.

and i will love you endlessly
and hopelessly
and heart-breakingly

and i will let you place footprints on my heart
walk over me for as long as you please
just don't walk away.

to my ex

i have tattoos you have never traced,
new scars you have never kissed,
grown out roots you have not stroked.
i have new favorite songs
and
new favorite books
and
new favorite people
and you are no longer one of them.

i have become a person you will never meet.
you do not deserve the pleasure.
i do not deserve the heartbreak.
(again.)

to my ex

i took the crumbs you gave me
convinced it was a whole loaf.

i was starving, you see?

no one had ever tried to feed me before
and i thought it was so romantic you did.
i gratefully grabbed on to the trail you left me,
happy i could feel the emptiness in me *slowly* being
replaced
by you.

i didn't realize it was crumbs until the end.
until i watched you take the bread out of your pocket
and give it all to her.
maybe she was more hungry than me.
maybe she deserved to be fed more than i did.

and i went back to starving.

to my ex

you promised me the world,
a ring on your favorite finger of mine,
a love that could never burn out.

i guess maybe that love was just never lit properly
in the first place
because as soon as you left,

you managed to light someone else up *so quickly.*
i was in pitch black
surrounded by nothing and darkness,

and i was alone.
i was so fucking alone.
so i tried to light myself,

for warmth,
when my own arms felt empty
and i burned myself to a crisp.

i destroyed whatever carcass you left of me
and ashes have never looked so ugly.
i've never felt so cold.

to my ex

"and here's the thing,
you just don't get to speak to me like that anymore,
okay?
it's not acceptable
and i'm sick of it.
so either change or leave,
because i refuse to spend another second begging you
to treat me the way you used to.
the way you should be."

is what i wanted to say.

instead,
i looked up at you,
eyes full of stupidity and love
and i said
"it's okay, baby.
i'm sorry i made you angry again."

to my ex

you are the sort of hurt that is
hand sanitizer on cuts
broken pinky toes
hangnails

you left me with
flowers wilting the day that i buy them
pens running out of ink
flat fizzy drinks

you made me feel like
night skies too cloudy to see the moon
bent cigarettes
abandoned stray cats

you told me we were
unmatched socks
creased bedding
unripe strawberries

you were destined to break my heart.

to
the
people
who
have
hurt
me

to the people who have hurt me

one man
told me he loved me
before we ever got
together.
i met his parents on the third date.
he met mine on the fourth.
he held my hand in public,
my face in private
and my heart in his hands always.
he gave me letters
and presents
and smiles
and hope.

he still cheated on me.

another man
kissed me on my forehead
before he ever even kissed my lips.
he boasted about me endlessly,
never touched my body hastily,
bought me flowers selflessly,
all just to see me smile.

he still screamed at me in the middle of my street.

another man
taught me young love,
loud, difficult, vibrant love.
he taught me how to kiss
and how to move my body
and how to hold hands.
he showed me the world,
and he kissed me
in every ocean.

he still assaulted me.

someone i am dating now
draws me pictures
and writes me letters.
he refuses to show me them yet.
he listens to shitty soundcloud remixes with me
and plays along with my weird games
and lets me drive us three towns over
just to escape for the night,
while we listen to a playlist he made for me.
i wonder what this man will do
and if i will even be surprised this time
when i find out he is another

almost good guy.

the letters i will never send

to the people who have hurt me

and today i burned you.
every part of you that still gripped onto me,
i pried off.
i finally let you go.
and oh,
you burned well,
all orange and brash,
the very last pieces of you
bellowing black smoke in my face.
i couldn't help but feel like this was the very last time
i'd let you blind me
or overpower me.

you burned like you existed,
out of control
and with no regard for anything around you.
you just engulfed whatever you could
in your own
destructive blaze
and ruined it.

i almost . . .
i almost let you ruin me.

so now you're ash,
gray and dizzying and gone,
swept up and discarded,
and i think,
finally—

finally i feel free.

to the people who have hurt me

the first words that left your mouth
when the time came
to raise our voices for the first time,
were about my weight.

i won't bore you with repeating it,
even in writing,
i think some things are better left unsaid.
it's just a shame that this is something
you were never taught.

for the next four weeks,
unbeknownst to you,
i ate only your unfulfilled promises
and starved myself on your love declarations.
i lost forty pounds and you said i'd never looked better.
i wondered if that was your plan all along.
it worked,
so i suppose i should be
grateful.

to the people who have hurt me

she was the sun's daughter,
full of fire and danger,
the sort of girl you couldn't stare at for too long
without sun-spotted vision and a headache.

her beauty was best observed from a distance,
but i didn't learn that until it was too late.

i loved her like i was the moon,
i revolved around her obediently,
quietly,
uneventfully but necessarily.

the issue was, though,
i tried to get too close
and she scorched me,
charred me,
until i was nothing but ruined rock and
broken self-esteem.

i miss her most days
but i miss more who i was before i met her.
i want that girl back again.
badly.

to the people who have hurt me

i will let you
lie about me.
i will let you
spread mistruths and
unkind things.
i will rise above it.

i will let you poison my name
and i will still
speak it clearly,
with pride.

i will coat my mouth in the truth
while you coat yours in
bitterness and jealousy.

so go ahead,
lie about me.

i will let you.

to the people who have hurt me

another friendship ruined,
another platonic heartbreak that hurts more than a
romantic one.
you broke my heart harder than any man ever has.
harder than the ones where we stayed up until 7am,
with you drying my tears
and feeding me chocolate.

i did the same for you,
drinking red wine
and swiping on tinder to show you
your ex was a piece of shit
(who really
was never that attractive in the first place).

you bought me more flowers than every boyfriend.
i hugged you tighter than anyone else.
we were family without blood
but i'd be a liar if i said i didn't bleed when you left.

i wrote you poems i never showed you
about how much you meant to me
and how much i adored you.
you wrote things about me, too,
you showed whoever you could,
but they weren't very nice things,
were they?

no,
thcy weren't.

to the people who have hurt me

you tell me i am
pretty.
i smile,
blush a little
and hope this might be the moment
i realize a man can love *me*
and not just *my body.*
i almost shiver in anticipation
for the reflection of our future
that i can see in your glasses.

then you say:
"and i'd love to see you laid out on my floor."

i wonder
if you want a girlfriend
or a lamb
to skin and craft a rug out of.

perhaps you find yourself attracted
to girls you can devour.
maybe you like to keep
small pieces of their bodies afterwards,
as trophies.
nude pictures and worn underwear and hair strands
stuck to unwashed pillowcases.

i contemplate the hidden meanings behind this;
the ownership kink;
the lack of healthy parental relationships
and the abandonment issues that led you here.
a therapist would probably adore digesting all of this.
the hunger you have for fresh meat.

i want to ask if you are starving,
but i know better than to pose silly questions to
men who cannot be held accountable for their actions.
hunger,

for those of you who don't know,
hunger seems to make men act differently.

you see, there is an unspoken rule about men with big
appetites
and women who can feed them.
you do,
and you don't fight back.
you leave them with a full belly
no matter how empty it makes you.
you let them feast on your body
make a meal out of your skin
and when they gnaw down to the bone
you let them lick it clean.

"on your floor?"
i question.
if i am to be devoured
do i not at least deserve
a table, washed hands, and silvered cutlery?

you wink at me.
"maybe on the bed,
if you're lucky."
and i think about how at least it is not in an alleyway,
like the last one.
i have only just recovered from being that man's dinner.
but at least you called me
pretty.

to the people who have hurt me

i
don't
think
i
quite
realized
what

insignificance

really
was,
until
i
met
you.

to the people who have hurt me

when we met for the first time,
on our first date
in a place too fancy to be called a bar,
you claimed the small of my back with your fingertips,
trailed down the sides of my waist
to my hips,
and took them as if they were yours now.

then you looked at ~~me~~ my body.
hung up in
metaphorical string
(like a carcass on a sunday)
and
literal ribbon
(like i belonged under a withering christmas tree).

you said i didn't need to dress as if my body had no
secrets,
that being in the presence of my mind
should be plenty enough.

i had never felt so seen
and so overlooked
all at once.
belittling and glorifying,
you didn't miss a beat as your eyes trailed over
everything my body seemed to scream.

"my body has secrets."
it was barely audible.
it was weak.
i grimaced as i said it.
i knew you wouldn't understand
(men like you never do),
and your eyes narrowed.
"good.
act like it."

you licked your lips
and it was as if your compliment
had been doused so deeply
in hidden meanings and male feminism,
i could see it dripping from
between your canines.

those teeth would later rip the ribbons right off of me.
i think we both liked to pretend that
it wasn't how the night would end
but there's an unspoken rule about
grown men like you
and
young girls like me.

you act as if you haven't taken
whatever you want from me.

i'll act as if i gave it to you.

to
my
body

some of the letters in this section
cover eating disorders, body dysmorphia, and self-harm.

if you are to send the letters in this chapter to
anyone, send them to those who will support
and understand you.

please use these letters to
reach out for help.

to my body

when i tell someone that i take cold showers, or paint
my nails every time i get hungry, or starve myself for
so long that i faint every time i stand up, i do not want
them to push me to recovery. i have no desire to get
better. part of the reason i tell them is because i want
that shocked expression, that worry, but with no real
consequences. the other part—secretly, deep down —the
one that makes me feel so fucked up and so guilty over,
is that i want a competitor. i want them to reply with
even worse habits, with ideas, with inspiration. i want
them to tell me how many days they've fasted for so i
can double it. i want them to tell me how much weight
they've lost so i realize that i've lost more. i want them
to compete with me, but lose. eating disorders should
not be competitive but believe me when i say, i am yet
to meet a "rexi" who doesn't burn with a rage so hot i
feel the heat radiating off of them every time they
realize they are not the skinniest person in the room.
i tell people sometimes because i am so proud of the
hurt i have caused myself,

*"look! look how badly i can treat my body! i bet you
can't do that, can you? have you? tell me, tell me
everything."*

i smell food instead of eating it, or chew and spit
instead of swallowing it. i will do everything i can to
stop those fucking calories from poisoning me. it is
exhilarating. so please, stare at me again and tell me i
have a problem. oh fuck. my body and i are so addicted
to concern.

to my body

i can't hold my body, touch it, stare at it
oh,
i will never understand how everyone else doesn't just
want to punch their reflection.
shatter that rectangular distorter into a million pieces,
give me all of the bad luck,
i mean—
i don't think the next seven years can get any worse
really.
and this body—
this body has done nothing wrong
and yet i punish it,
send it to bed without dinner,
make it sit in isolation,
critique every lump and bump and crevice.
i do not think there is a single part
of my body
that i can say
i love,
i cannot even use the word "like."
"tolerate"
comes to mind,
but even then,
the pain i cause myself
is not particularly tolerant.

to my body

i had a sandwich today.	*that means i'm getting better! right?*
cheese and red onion chutney.	*and i'm allowed to eat cheese now, right?*
i stuffed it with salad until i thought it might not close.	*because salad has like, zero calories. right?*
i drank a liter of water while i ate it.	*it's good to drink water while i eat . . . right?*
and i used two whole slices of bread for the sandwich!	*sorry. i know you don't like it when i eat bread.*
that's two more than i had yesterday,	*are you angry with me for recovering?*
or the day before that.	*i know, i miss you, too.*
i had some olives on the side	*but i hated how you made me feel.*
and i didn't even pat them dry with a paper towel	*i can't keep listening to you telling me what to do.*
before eating them this time.	*i don't want to be starving forever.*
there was butter on both bits of bread,	*i know you just want what's best for me,*
i mean, it was thin,	*but please stop screaming at me,*
but it was there,	*i just want to get better. we can't keep doing this.*
barely existing.	*i have to learn to exist without you, i'm sorry.*

afterwards,
 i slept.
exhausted.

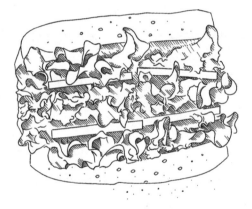

to my body

there's this mirror,
opposite my shower.
a rectangular reflector that seems to warp my body
into a pink fleshy blob,
thighs so dimpled
they resemble the surface of the moon
and a stomach that shakes like those shitty little jellies
we used to get given as kids.
you know, the ones that barely held together,
no substance to them, no real taste either,
just this mess of color and wobbles.
i didn't ever eat the jelly anyway,
way too much sugar,
way too many calories.

and if i stare into this mirror long enough,
while i wash myself,
hands avoiding body parts i refuse to let
even myself touch,
i begin to wonder if my reflection in his eyes is the
same as this one,
if those wide hazel eyes see what i see.
the lumps, the discoloration, the wobbles.
i wonder if he sees jelly, too.
i wonder if he is
as disgusted as i am.

one day—
one day i will smash that mirror.

to my body

and i don't just want to be skinny.
the sort where you have your life together
and go to hot yoga classes,
have oat milk lattes after,
and giggle about drinking
all the calories you just burned.

i want people to worry about me,
i want hugs that last a little bit too long
where they trace every bone in my back with a hand
that screams of disgust.
i want to be the sort of skinny
where it hurts to get out of bed again,
where my lips are always a little bit chapped
and my eyes look a bit too glass-like.
i want the sort of skinny
that goes hand in hand with black lungs
and yellowed teeth.
i miss having to paint my nails
to hide the discoloration.

i think i want to be unhealthy skinny again.
i want to feast on the concern others hold for me,
engulf every last eye widen at my naked body,
taste the way they are uncomfortable to be around me.
i so miss the way they used to tell me i had a problem,
i miss pretending to eat,
and hiding my workouts.
two hundred sit-ups with a pillow beneath me,

a fifteen-minute butterfly stretch
before i can eat anything,
a cold shower for as long as i can last
and no towel allowed after.
oh,
it's fucking insane.

and i have to stop now,
because i do not want anyone
to mistake this poem as a
manual,
a guide of how to become sick,
i do not want to be held responsible for anyone's death
but my own.
i cannot allow someone to beat me at my own game.

these habits have been coded into me, i have grown
among them and around them,
they are entangled into me.
i will never stop wanting
to go back to how i used to be,
i ache for it.
and i can see it killing me one day,
i think it's easier to let myself carry on down the rabbit
hole than it is to stop,
the only difference being i wouldn't dare eat that cake
like alice did.

to my body

my body is pleading with me
for crumbs of self-love.

it is begging me for some sort of acknowledgment,
for at least a compromised existence.

but my body
is just not deserving of anything
but disgust.

to my body

"boys don't likes fat girls,"
is what my mother told me as she took me to
my first diet class.
i was fourteen
and i didn't think i would ever like anyone,
let alone worry about them liking me,
but five years on,
when i have come to realize that her statement
was nothing but an ugly truth,
i spend my evenings recluse,
hiding from skinny girls
and the boys that like them.
i stopped attending diet classes a long time ago.
it is rare i am hit on now,
it is even rarer that it is done not as a joke,
and so,
because i am a punchline,
because no one likes fat girls
(not even the fat girl herself),
whenever someone *does* hit on me,
i will do whatever they want.
no questions asked.
fat beggars cannot be choosers.

to my body

my body does not define me.
full.
fucking.
stop.
i define me.

to
my
therapist

some of the letters in this section cover
mental health and trauma.

your therapist might be a friend, a partner, a
mother. there is more to this title than just
a university degree.

use these letters to reach out
for help, support, and love.

to my therapist

i don't know who i am without mental illness,

but i so wish i did.

to my therapist

my light switch
is so far away.

i can see it,
taunting me across the valleys of my bedroom.
i just can't break the distance between us.
i don't have the energy to make such a trip
and so it stares at me.

sometimes
it really looks like it's snarling at me,
like it's jeering at me.
i think it must know
i am too sick of living to be surrounded by brightness,
but too new to dying to be comfortable in darkness.

i fall asleep with the light on.
when i wake, exhausted from sleeping,
i sit up before deciding
today is not the day to make such a voyage.
i lie back down,
and i dream of flicking the light switch off.

tomorrow, perhaps.

to my therapist

i'm not being hurt anymore,
or abused,
but i am still acting like i am.

i cannot shake the comfort of
victimhood.

i do not know who i am without it.

there is a home in my trauma,
in how my brain cannot process safety.

i miss being traumatized.
it is masochistic,
i know,
but it is beautifully home to me.

without fear,
i am not sure how to exist.

i am just floating uncomfortably through life

with "victim" branded across my heart
and "broken" carved into my soul.

to my therapist

my body was made to be fucked.
my mind is begging to be loved.

i am yet to meet someone who acts on the latter.

to my therapist

i don't think anyone quite gets it.
they pretend to, sure.
they act like they're sympathizing with me,
they try to see why i feel so broken,
but they don't *really* understand how it feels.

i have ripped my own heart out of my chest,
i have convinced my brain to hate itself,
i have hurt myself until pain
is the only company i feel safe in.
they don't get me.

and it is so fucking hard
explaining all of this to people
while they look at me with puppy dog eyes
and hold me in pity hugs.

i think i would rather suffer in silence
and so i do.

i don't tell a soul.

to my therapist

i'm just so sick of living.
i'm trying so hard to escape this feeling
but no matter how far i run
or how much i empty my lungs
i cannot out-chase the desire
of wishing i didn't exist.

and sometimes,
(a lot of the time),
i find it hard to breathe,
like i am too crowded by nothing to fill my chest,
like the air has been stolen from me.
i don't know who by,
because to be honest
it's not as if there is anyone close to me.
most days i am lonely in my aloneness
and unequivocally begging to not be.
i miss breathing deeply.
i miss living properly.
i miss not being alone.

to my therapist

it was always my best-kept secret.
some women pretended they didn't have botox,
others that they could afford the designer clothes they
bought every weekend,
a few that they were happy in their marriages.

i pretended i didn't want to die every day.
that my closet wasn't so full with skeletons
it couldn't close,
that i could leave my bed every day without
feeling the need to sink back in as soon as i left.

i wish my secret was so mundane and
repetitive on the ears.
but it's not.
it's ugly
and it's real
and it will forever be *my* secret.

i don't know what the fuck is wrong with me
because i can't seem to get better.
i do think i want to,
i just don't know how to function normally anymore,
living is just *too much* for me.

i've always been good at keeping secrets.
i think i will take this one to the grave.
(hopefully.)

to my therapist

i think i must be attracted
to all of the things that
i am not.

the way they are effortlessly beautiful
and kind
and sweet-natured.

i wish i possessed
those feminine qualities
instead of my own,

and so i wonder
if i have ever
actually loved a woman properly

or maybe, i hated myself so badly
i loved what i wished i was.
if i have only ever loved

what i am not.

to my therapist

there's beauty in being a survivor
and not because

"my trauma made me stronger."

that's bullshit.

that's the sort of shit men say so they feel deserving
of leering at you for a little bit longer.
it's the sort of shit people say before they
demand to hear your story
and make you regurgitate your victimhood
into their hands.

the beauty of being a survivor comes from

*"i have found comfort with other survivors and i know
we are not alone."*

it's the sort of friendship you never wanted,
but are grateful to now have.

this is the sort of shit you say, you feel,
this is not like those words that have been shoved into
    your mouth by non-victims
(like there hasn't been enough forced onto you
already).

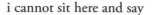

i cannot sit here and say

"my trauma made me stronger,"

because it did not.
i did have to make myself stronger,
but rest assured i was fine beforehand.
i didn't birth my strength from weakness.
being a victim
is not weakness

and your victimhood is no one's but your own.

to
other
poets

to other poets

to write is to transcribe yourself.
to be held in the palms of a stranger and reveal yourself
page by page
as they flip through your trauma
and your unspeakables.
it is the creation of a bond between reader and writer
that goes far beyond any other connection in existence.
it is pure
and scary
and completely unfiltered
and it is the best relationship you will ever create.
so, my child,

write.

to other poets

i write this sitting in the rain.
if i were clever enough,
i would draft up a few lines
explaining how the weather reflects my thoughts.
how i am as alone as each droplet seems to be.
i think, maybe,
my english teacher might be proud of me
for remembering techniques like that
but then again
i almost failed her class
so i'm sure she'd be somewhat content
with me remembering
anything she tried to teach me.

it's dark out.
it's still raining.
it's 12:02.
i am shivering,
and i can't quite put my finger
on why my face is so wet.
i think at some point i lost track of where
the rain starts
(and the words flow)
and i end
(and the lines begin)
and i think perhaps
(perhaps)
that is for the best.

to other poets

i am not a poet.
i am a twenty-year-old girl
who cries more often than smiling.
i am nothing but a girl who pretends
to be in touch
with my emotions, but is such an open book,
most people recognize what i am feeling
long before i do.

i am a constant whirlwind of confusion
for myself and for anyone else
unlucky enough to be caught up in my storm.

i am a young adult completely lost in life,
with a hundred maps in my car's central console
and i am too scared to pick one to follow.

i am not a poet,
but i am an emotional wreck who writes to escape
decision-making and processing my feelings.
it is the only thing that puts me to sleep
and wakes me up the next morning.

i write,
or
word vomit,
whatever you want to call it,
just to cope.

i am not a poet.
i am not keats, or wilde, or shakespeare, or plath.
i am not living to write.
i am writing to live.

perhaps one day i can write
without the need to be saved.

to other poets

my dating profile states
that i am looking
for a fellow poet.
what it doesn't say
is this:

i would quite like
for us
to write each other
into eternal existence.

i would quite like
for us
to spend the rest of our lives
imprinting ink stains
onto each other's skin.

i would quite like
for us
to hope that our words will only ever fade
when the pages are bleached with sunlight and our ink
finally runs dry.

what i would love though,
what i really am
"looking for,"
on an app

where my body is your only talking point
and the opening messages you send
tell me i'd look prettier
laid out on your floor,

is to never have to write a poem
about my broken heart
ever
again.
i wish to fix her for good.

to other poets

sometimes i wish writing had never
found me,
that i had coping mechanisms other than
regurgitation.

but i do not.

sometimes i wish hopeless romanticism had never
poisoned me,
that i had pure dreams other than
infatuation.

but i do not.

sometimes i wish other people had never
broken me,
that i had self-projections other than
commiseration.

but i do not.

heart-wrenchingly
desperate
to be.

heart-achingly
unfortunately
not.

to other poets

after i had begun to drown in my own poetry, in the words that i was forced to birth from your cruelty, i realized that swimming seemed far more difficult than i had first anticipated.

perhaps healing would be, too.

i pleaded for arm bands in the form of full stops, or new beginnings, and air tanks that could inflate me like
       your
words of affirmation used to.

i hoped for a new muse or a new purpose to write of, although i found myself only attracted to writing prompts not too dissimilar from you.

when i tried to write of something else, someone else, an awful lot of the lines still looked like you. when i'd step back and squint at the pages, i'd find you between the ink spills and the blank spaces. i had never realized before how empty my work looks when it is not talking of you, how the gaps between words seem to scream your name so angrily in your absence.

it is as if my pages know only you. i am beginning to forget how they looked before i began to transcribe you. i cannot remember if they were always this empty or if i just miss you so terribly, i have embodied my deprivation of you into the only place i can.

i suppose it makes sense. my poetry is now the only place i can recognize you in. or rather, i should say, it is the only place i can recognize the you i thought i knew in.

to other poets

you were given powerful words
for a reason,
my darling,
so use them.
tell your story,
i promise i am not the only one waiting to read it.
the world is waiting to listen to you,
open-eared and open-hearted.
tell us what has happened to you.
write about it.
speak about it.
tell the mirror,
tell me,
tell the world.
just make sure you tell somebody,
even if for now it is just a blank piece of paper and a pen.
it is a start.
and we are waiting for you.

to other poets

if i do not write, i think i might just stop breathing. my
fingertips are bruised and my palms are calloused and
my lover kisses them softer. my lungs are filling with
liquid emotions and i am afraid of what may happen if i
do not expel them into my work.
i say:
> *"i must tell my story to anyone with ears."*

my lover says:

> *"ears do not mean they will listen."*

and he kisses my hands all over, until i place my pen
down and pick up his heart. i look at him wide-eyed as
if it will help me to see all of him and am met with a
face that knows why my soul is shaking. the only time i
feel alive is in his arms.
i say:
> *"but it is all i know."*

my lover says:

> *"then let me teach you what you do not."*

to other poets

poetry

is the
healthiest addiction
i have
ever held.

to

past

me

to past me

our life does get better.

trust me.

i made sure of it.

to past me

i know how sick you are of hearing the words:
"you're beautiful,"
but believe me when i tell you
it does not mean your worth
is belittled into how your face is shaped.

the slope of your nose
speaks to the curves of your soul.
the fullness of your lips
mimics the heaviness of your heart.
the brightness of your eyes
copies the clarity of your mind.

being told you are pretty
is not a trade-off with being intelligent.
you must know you are
smart and funny and kind-hearted.
you must know this is real.

you are content being the funny friend,
the smart girl in the back of the classroom,
but believe me,
it is okay to be beautiful, too.
it is okay to let yourself soften slightly
with the kind words others have offered you.

open the corners of your heart and allow their
compliments to engulf your edges
until they have rounded.

you will not lose yourself to your beauty,
you can claim it as your own
without forfeiting you.
you can acknowledge your beauty as others do
and still know that you are so much more.

to past me

i'm sorry to say,
we didn't end up with our prince charming.
we didn't even end up with the frog.
it pains me to tell you this but
they didn't want you either,
my darling.

but i promise you
they did us a favor.
you're alone,
but you're happy.
you are content in your own company
and it's good.
you're really good.

someone *will* come along one day,
i'm sure of it.
we are so damn lovable,
even on days where we write poems about
how we are not.

but we won't compromise
or yearn for them,
no,
we will wait patiently
and silently

and happily.

to past me

my heart still hurts
when i think about how terribly i treated you.
i do not think i will ever forgive myself
for the pain
and the self-loathing
and the hatred—
so hot, my insides burned.

it was a fire made up of detestation that i started.
so unruly and so out of control,
i let it engulf you.
i resented you.
i cannot honestly say that i have managed to
extinguish the flames,
but i have learned to stop feeding them.

you will learn to love yourself,
perhaps not every day, and not every bit,
but those stretch marks fade
into slithers of silver that decorate your hips:
your cellulite is braille that you let only him read;
the scars you carry
are now proudly worn badges.
memories of both good and bad,
but they make you
you.

it will not happen overnight
and i know you wish it would,
but this journey to self-appreciation
is going to be simultaneously the most difficult
and most rewarding thing you are yet to do.

you are still so young
and i am so sorry for all the hurt i have caused
but it will get better.
we *will* get better.

to past me

and those girls,
the ones who made your life hell?
they come back.
they ask me for your forgiveness
they watch us succeed
and you'll want me to shove it in their faces.
but i won't.
you know what i'll do?
smile and say thank you.
they broke you and you fixed yourself
so that i could smile in their faces
and walk away knowing it was all worth it
it was the *"character development"*
<u>we never deserved,</u>
but we learned to accept and love anyway.

to past me

i would do anything for you
most nights i dream of wiping your tears
and holding you tight
if time travel were possible
i'd rip every hole in the fabric of space
just to comfort you
to help you see your worth
because we are worth a hell of a lot
i know you don't realize it now
but you will
soon.

to past me

your life is not a montage.
you have to live the boring bits in between
but i promise you,
it makes the good bits feel like so much more.

to past me

i cannot begin to express how apologetic i am for the
next few years. i want you to try to be brave. you are
going to grow up so quickly and you are going to have
to be the glue that holds your family together when
everything else around you is crumbling. you are going
to mourn a parent that decided to leave you, even if he
was never really a parent to begin with. you're going to
speak to so many new adults and they will ask you so
many questions you do not know the answers to, but
they will keep asking anyway. be truthful—i know how
scary it all seems but it will help in the long run. your
mum is going to cry (a lot), so let her. try not to
cry yourself though, not around her anyway. just hold her,
and be kind. it will get easier.

there's nothing i can say to prevent it but i know how
you feel about your body and i know the rabbit hole
you are about to fall down. you stay there for a long
time, but i will be there, hanging over the side, arms
outstretched and reaching for you, waiting to pull you
out. you poor child, i cannot sugarcoat this, you will
struggle. you are too young for the hurt you will
experience and it will stay with you, but it is the very
reason we will become the girl who envelops others in
an unconditional love.

you are going to heal others and inspire thousands. you are going to do everything you wish someone would have done for you but trust me, this is so much more fulfilling.

you are going to do amazing things and become a person you are *proud to be*.

to past me

when you think no one loves you,
remember this:
i still look at pictures of you,
pray that self-love had found you sooner,
and adore you more than enough for the both of us.
that is plenty.
i promise.

you are more beautiful than you think
and you turn out so damn kind.
(i like to think anyway)
and that is all that matters.

people will learn to love you
as i did,
because i really do
i love you.
i love us.

to
future
me

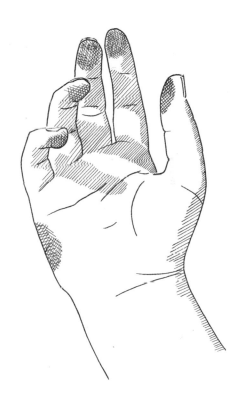

to future me

i pray that you are the best version of me yet, that you have acquired new freckles from a summer romance with the sun. i hope you have experienced the world through sun-spotted vision and witnessed sunsets with colors that rival your next lover's eyes.

i pray that the skin around your mouth is more wrinkled and puckered from happiness, that it shows we have lived a life of fulfillment and felicity.

i pray that you have not fallen back into our old habits of feeling empty and of pushing everyone away. there is no more room in our lives for other loved ones to leave (unless, of course, we ask them to).

i pray that your cheeks know no tears, that you have tasted every last bit of salt until you have no appetite for seasonings other than peppery happiness.

i pray that you get out of bed every morning (or at least try to), even on days where the sunlight gives you a headache and your curtains are screaming to remain closed.

i pray that you have not become a shell of yourself again, but in the likelihood that you have, you must promise me that you will try to recover the pieces of you that are missing.

i pray that you heal, that you make every crevice of our body ache with how deep the therapist prods. you cannot stop trying to fix what i broke.

i pray that we will do something with our life. i know that we have lived through and dealt with too much for this to be it.

i pray that you are okay. i pray just that we are content.

to future me

there are still days where
i succumb to the damage others have caused,
but i am working on it.

i am learning to love myself again,
scars and all.

i know they tell my story
and i am excited to carry on reading.

to future me

i like the slope of my nose,
i like how my eyes are a little too close together,
i like how my hair part is never quite in the middle.

i'm starting to like my insecurities again.
and wholeheartedly
i think it is the best thing i have ever done.

i'm falling back in love with myself.
slowly,
but i am falling nonetheless.

the letters i will never send

to future me

perhaps my mental illness is not
just
who i am,

but what i learned to heal.

to future me

three hundred and sixty-four days
are waiting to be conquered by you.
and if this one
forces you to surrender,
then so be it.
tomorrow will be yours for the taking.

your
letters

your letters

these pages are for you. write your own letters. tear them out. burn them. send them.

just make sure you do something with them.

to
from

the letters i will never send

to

from

the letters i will never send

to

from

the letters i will never send

to

from

the letters i will never send

to
from

the letters i will never send

221

to

from

the letters i will never send

to
from

the letters i will never send

225

to

from

the letters i will never send

about the author

isabella dorta is a bestselling author. she self-published her first book on valentine's day 2022. as a true victim of heartbreak and love, her poetry is birthed from real life and tells isabella's story.

known for reading her poetry aloud on social media, isabella refers to herself not as a poet, but as a young woman who just feels things "a little too ferociously." she posted her first poem online in may 2021 and has since built a loving community of followers who have given isabella a platform to continue sharing her poetry.

@isabelladortapoetry444
on tiktok and instagram.

other work by the author

how sunflowers bloom under moonlight

acknowledgments

please excuse me, and my loud heart;

sometimes, she beats so furiously, i forget to thank the people that have helped her to heal. i am working on this so *this is me not forgetting.*

thank you to sam, the most wonderful and patient editor i could have ever hoped to work with. i can't put into words how brilliant you've been. thank you for guiding me through the scary world of publishing with so much kindness.

thank you to the rest of the amazingly talented people who have helped bring this book to life. i've worked with a lot of lovely people in the past, but nothing compares to you all.

thank you to the people i have dedicated chapters to, even the not-so-nice ones. thank you for feeding my passion for healing, i hope you read this book regretfully and i hope you know which poems contain your silent names.

thank you to my dear friends and family; my mother, my brother, lukas, orianna, charley, donovan, and any others who i may find in the future. i owe you everything. you are the softest and sweetest beings i have ever met.

thank you to you, my dear reader, for understanding and reading my transcribed inner workings. i'll never not be grateful for the opportunity to word vomit my personal experiences into poetry. thank you for being gentle with me and holding me in your palms carefully.

thank you to the existence of social media; you're *sort of the worst,* but without you i would not be able to call myself an author. thank you for allowing me to put some good back into the universe and the platforms we are all so addicted to.

finally, my largest thank you is owed to persian queen atossa, for creating my lifelong, favorite form of communication. a queen at 28, she sent the first ever recorded letter in 500bc. for this, i owe her an unspeakable amount of gratefulness. thank you for allowing me to fall in love; to record my happiness and my downfalls; to numb my fingertips as well as my mind; to heal happily and healthily. thank you, atossa. thank you.